Hawks

Picture research by Ian Wyles

Printed and bound in Great Britain by
Hazell Watson & Viney Ltd, Aylesbury
for the Publishers, W. H. Allen & Co. Ltd,
44 Hill Street, London W1X 8LB

ISBN 0 491 02761 5

Hawks

Edited by
Lynn Hughes

WH Allen · London
A Howard & Wyndham Company
1981

He clasps the crag with crooked hands;
Close to the sun in lonely lands,
Ring'd with the azure world, he stands.
The wrinkled sea beneath him crawls;
He watches from his mountain walls,
And like a thunderbolt he falls.

TENNYSON
THE EAGLE

'Call down the hawk from the air;
Let him be hooded or caged
Till the yellow eye has grown mild,
For larder and spit are bare,
The old cook enraged,
The scullion gone wild.'
'I will not be clapped in a hood,
Nor a cage, nor alight upon wrist,
Now I have learnt to be proud
Hovering over the wood
In the broken mist
Or tumbling cloud.'
'What tumbling cloud did you cleave,
Yellow-eyed hawk of the mind,
Last evening? that I, who had sat
Dumbfounded before a knave,
Should give to my friend
A pretence of wit.'

W. B. YEATS
THE HAWK

The Element of air is most properly mine, I and my Hawks use that most, and it yields us most recreation. It stops not the high soaring of my noble, generous Falcon; in it she ascends to such a height, as the dull eyes of beasts and fish are not able to reach to; their bodies are too gross for such high elevations; in the Air my troops of Hawks soar up on high, and when they are lost in the sight of men, then they attend upon the converse with the Gods; therefore I think my Eagle is so justly styled Jove's servant in ordinary: and that very Falcon, that I am now going to see, deserves no meaner a title, for she usually in her flight endangers herself, like the son of Daedalus, to have her wings scorched by the sun's heat, she flies so near it, but her mettle makes her careless of danger; for she then heeds nothing but makes her nimble pinions cut the fluid air, and so makes her highway over the steepest mountains and deepest rivers, and in her glorious career looks with contempt upon those high steeples and magnificent palaces which we adore and wonder at; from which height, I can make her to descend by a word from my mouth, which she both knows and obeys, to accept of meat from my hand, to own me for her Master, to go home with me, and be willing the next day to afford me the like recreation.

ISAAC WALTON
THE COMPLEAT ANGLER

I caught this morning morning's minion, king-
dom of daylight's dauphin, dapple-dawn-drawn
Falcon, in his riding
Of the rolling level underneath him steady air, and
striding
High there, how he rung upon the rein of a wimpling
wing
In his ecstasy! then off, off forth on swing,
As a skate's heel sweeps smooth on a bow-bend: the
hurl and gliding
Rebuffed the big wind. My heart in hiding
Stirred for a bird, - the achieve of, the mastery of the
thing!
Brute beauty and valour and act, oh, air, pride, plume,
here
Buckle! AND the fire that breaks from thee then, a
billion
Times told lovelier, more dangerous, O my chevalier!
No wonder of it: shéer plód makes plough down
sillion
Shine, and blue-bleak embers, ah my dear,
Fall, gall themselves, and gash gold-vermilion.

GERARD MANLEY HOPKINS
THE WINDHOVER

With empty hand nae man should hawks allure.

SCOTTISH PROVERB

Gos generally looked terrible, terrible in the sense that an eagle or a vulture had that look. In the strong sunlight which shone on the lake - at last the weather was pretending to turn for haymaking - he certainly looked beautiful. But the cruelty had gone out of his aspect. He was only a funny and silly little Gos, whose transparent mind showed him to be an infant still, as it struggled with the elements of hydrostatics. The sun shone on him, giving him a blue nimbus round his head. The cere flesh about his nostrils was supposedly yellow, as were the irises of his eyes. But that luminous eye (his main feature; it glared out, a focus to all the rest of him, from under frowning brow, the optic of an insane assassin) was genuinely luminous, like the paint on the hands of a wrist-watch. Luminous paint, phosphorus: it was blue really, just as much as it was yellow. So the sunlight on Gos took a blue tinge from the hairy whiskers which he wore about his cere and eyelid, carried it on to the eye itself, haloed the whole head in a tint exquisitely elusive, of bird flesh - neither blue nor yellow.

T. H. WHITE
THE GOSHAWK

Falco palumbarius Lin. Der Stockfalke Mas

This high-caught hooded Reason broods upon my
wrist,
Fettered by a so tenuous leash of steel.
We are bound for the myrtle marshes, many leagues
away,
And have a fair expectation of quarry.
Over the laggard dove, inclining to green boscage
Hovers this intentional doom - till the unsullied sky
receives
A precipitation of shed feathers
And the swifter fall of wounded wings.
Will the plain aye echo with that loud *hullallo!*
Or retain an impress of our passage?
We have caught Beauty in a wild foray
And now the falcon is hooded and comforted
away.

HERBERT READE
THE FALCON AND THE DOVE

FALCO CANDICANS, *J.F. Gmel.*

Greenland Falcon, light race adult and young

There is a species of hawk known as the Kestrel which has no need whatever to drink. Another species is the Orites Hawk. Both species are remarkably addicted to the female bird and pursue it after the manner of lovesick men and never cease from the pursuit. But should the female chance to disappear without the male noticing it, he is overcome with grief and cries aloud and is like one in the depths of woe from love. When Hawks are troubled with their eyesight they go straight to some stone wall and pull up some wild lettuce and then holding it above their eyes allow the bitter, astringent juice to drip in; and this restores their health. And men say that doctors use them in various ways.

CLAUDIUS AELIANUS
ON ANIMALS

The Vulture eats between his meals,
  And that's the reason why
He very, very rarely feels
  As well as you and I.
His eye is dull, his head is bald,
  His neck is growing thinner.
Oh! what a lesson for us all
  To only eat at dinner!

HILAIRE BELLOC
THE VULTURE

Vulture. A sluggish, ungenerous race; prey oftner on dead animals, and even putrid carcases, than on living creatures. Their sense of smelling most exquisite. Collect in flocks from afar; directed to their prey by the sagacity of their nostrils. Fly slowly and heavily. Are most greedy, and voracious to a proverb. Are not timid, for they prey in the midst of cities, undaunted by mankind.

THOMAS PENNANT
GENERA OF BIRDS

Le Vautour fauve

Over Sir John's Hill,
The hawk on fire hangs still;
In a hoisted cloud, at drop of dusk, he pulls to his
claws
And gallows, up the rays of his eyes the small birds
of the bay
And the shrill child's play
Wars
Of the sparrows and such who swansing, dusk, in
wrangling hedges.
And blithely they squawk
To fiery tyburn over the wrestle of elms until
The flash the noosed hawk
Crashes, and slowly the fishing holy stalking heron
In the river Towy below bows his tilted headstone.
Flash, and the plumes crack,
And a black cap of jack-
Daws Sir John's just hill dons, and again the
gulled birds hare
To the hawk on fire, the halter height, over
Towy's fins,
In a whack of wind.
There
Where the elegiac fisherbird stabs and paddles
In the pebbly dab-filled
Shallow and sedge, and 'dilly dilly,' calls the loft
hawk,
'Come and be killed.'

DYLAN THOMAS
OVER SIR JOHN'S HILL

At eleven o'clock the tiercel peregrine flew steeply up above the river, arching and shrugging his wings into the gale, dark on the grey clouds racing over. Wild peregrines love the wind, as otters love water. It is their element. Only within it do they truly live. All wild peregrines I have seen have flown longer and higher and further in a gale than at any other time. They avoid it only when bathing or sleeping. The tiercel glided at two hundred feet, spread his wings and tail upon the billowing air, and turned down wind in a long and sweeping curve. Quickly his circles stretched away to the east, blown out elliptically by the force of the wind. Hundreds of birds rose beneath him. The most exciting thing about a hawk is the way in which it can create life from the still earth by conjuring flocks of birds into the air. All the feeding gulls and lapwings and woodpigeons went up from the big field between the road and the brook as the hawk circled above them. The farm seemed to be hidden by a sheet of white water, so close together were the rising gulls. Dark through the white gulls the sharp hawk dropped, shattering them apart like flinging white foam.

J. A. BAKER
THE PEREGRINE

The *Falcon* charges at first view
With her brigade of Talons; through
Whose Shoots, the wary *Heron* beat,
With a well counterwheel'd retreat.
The desp'rate *Heron* now contracts,
In one design all former facts;
Noble he is resolv'd to fall
His, and his En'mies funerall,
And (to be rid of her) to dy
A publick Martyr of the Sky.
When now he turns his last to wreak
The palizadoes of his Beak;
The raging foe impatient
Wrack'd with revenge, and fury rent,
Swift as the Thunderbolt he strikes,
Too sure upon the stand of Pikes,
There she his naked breast doth hit
And on the case of Rapiers's split.
But ev'n in her expiring pangs
The *Heron's* pounc'd within her Phangs,
And so above she stoops to rise
A Trophee and a Sacrifice;
Whilst her own Bells in the sad fall
Ring out the double Funerall.

RICHARD LOVELACE
THE FALCON

I sit in the top of the wood, my eyes closed.
Inaction, no falsifying dream
Between my hooked heat and hooked feet:
Or in sleep rehearse perfect kills and eat.
The convenience of the high trees!
The air's buoyancy and the sun's ray
Are of advantage to me;
And the earth's face upward for my inspection.
My feet are locked upon the rough bark.
It took the whole of Creation
To produce my foot, my each feather:
Now I hold Creation in my foot
Or fly up, and revolve it all slowly -
I kill where I please because it is all mine.
There is no sophistry in my body:
My manners are tearing off heads -
The allotment of death.
For the one path of my flight is direct
Through the bones of the living.
No arguments assert my right:
The sun is behind me.
Nothing has changed since I began.
My eye has permitted no change.
I am going to keep things like this.

TED HUGHES
HAWK ROOSTING

FALCO CHERRUG . CHERRUG FALCON.

Suddenly the rook closes its wings, and drops like a stone towards the village. Instantly the falcon is round, and poising herself a moment, drives at the falling rook in a headlong oblique stoop. She cleaves the air like a meteor, and is below and up to the rook with the quickness of thought. Both birds appear for the fraction of a second to come together, the rook makes a twisting dive, the falcon shoots perpendicularly upwards, and a puff of black feathers is left in the air. It has been a narrow shave for the rook, but he continues to drop towards the trees which are now immediately below him, while the falcon turns over, and shoots down vertically behind him, with all the force she can muster. Fortune, however, this time favours the rook, who saves himself in one last desperate shift, and takes refuge among the trees of the rookery which has been his point from the first. The baffled falcon cruises about over the tree-tops, greeted by a noisy and defiant chorus of cawing from the rookery.

GILBERT BLAINE
FALCONRY

LESSER PEREGRINE.

FALCO MINOR

Whoever shall take the eyrie of a hawk, let him pay a pound to the king. The worth of a red hawk before it be put in a mew is half a pound; after it is taken from the mew, being white, its value is a pound. The worth of a male hawk is twenty-four pence. The eyrie of a sparrow-hawk is twenty-four pence in value; when red it is twelve pence in value; if it be white when taken out of the mew, it is twenty-four pence in value.

HYWEL DDA
THE LAW (10th Century)

As when a cast of faulcons make their flight,
At an herneshaw that lyes aloft on wing
The whyles they strike at him with heedlesse might
The warie foule his bill doth backward wring,
On which the first, whose force her first doth bring
Herselfe quite through the bodie, doth engore
And falleth downe to ground like senselesse thing,
But th' other, not so swift as she before,
Fayles of her souse, and passing by doth hurt no more.

SPENSER
FAERIE QUEEN

We have ospraies, which breed with us in parks and woods, whereby the keepers of the same doo reape in breeding time no small commoditie; for so soone almost as the yoong are hatched, they tie them to the but ends or ground ends of sundrie trees, where the old ones finding them, doo never cease to bring fish unto them which the keepers take and eat from them, and commonlie is such as is well fed, not of the worst sort. It hath not beene my hap hitherto to see anie of these foules, and partlie through mine owne negligence: but I heare that it hath one foot like an hawke to catch hold withall, and another resembling a goose wherewith to swim; but whether it be so, or not so, I refer the further search and trial thereof to some other.'

HOLINSHED
CHRONICLE

The Kite is sometimes called the glead; though in the English translation of Deuteronomy xiv. 13, glede and kite are mentioned separately. According to Belon, who wrote about the year 1560, an amazing number of kites used to collect in the streets of London for the sake of the refuse which was thrown into the gutters. People were forbidden to kill them, and the birds were so tame that they took their prey in the midst of the greatest crowds, after the manner of pigeons in our time. Their familiarity, however, was not quite so harmless, for they occasionally invaded the butchers' stalls and helped themselves to what they fancied.

EMMA PHIPSON
THE ANIMAL-LORE OF
SHAKESPEARE'S TIME

A peculiar remedy the Ancients had against the consumption of Hawks. For, filling a Chicken with Vinegar, they closed up the Bill, and hanging it up untill the Flesh grew tender, they fed the Hawk therewith: and to restore and well Flesh them, they commonly gave them Hogs Flesh, with Oil, Butter and Honey; and a decoction of Cumfory to bouze; and had a notable medicine against the inflammation of the eyes, by juice of purslain, opium, and saffron. They disallowed of salt Meats and Fat; but highly esteemed of Mice in most indispositions; and in the falling Sickness had great esteem of boiled Batts: and in many Diseases, of the Flesh of Owls which fed upon those Animals. In Epilepsies they also gave the Brain of a Kid drawn thorough a gold Ring; and, in Convulsions, made use of a mixture of Musk and *Stercus humanum aridum.* For the better preservation of their Health they strowed Mint and Sage about them; and for the speedier mewing of their Feathers, they gave them the Slough of a Snake, or a Tortoise out of the Shell, or a green Lizard cut in pieces. If a Hawk were unquiet, they hooded him, and placed him in a Smith's Shop for some time, where, accustomed to the continual noise of hammering, he became more gentle and tractable.

SIR THOMAS BROWNE
TRACTS

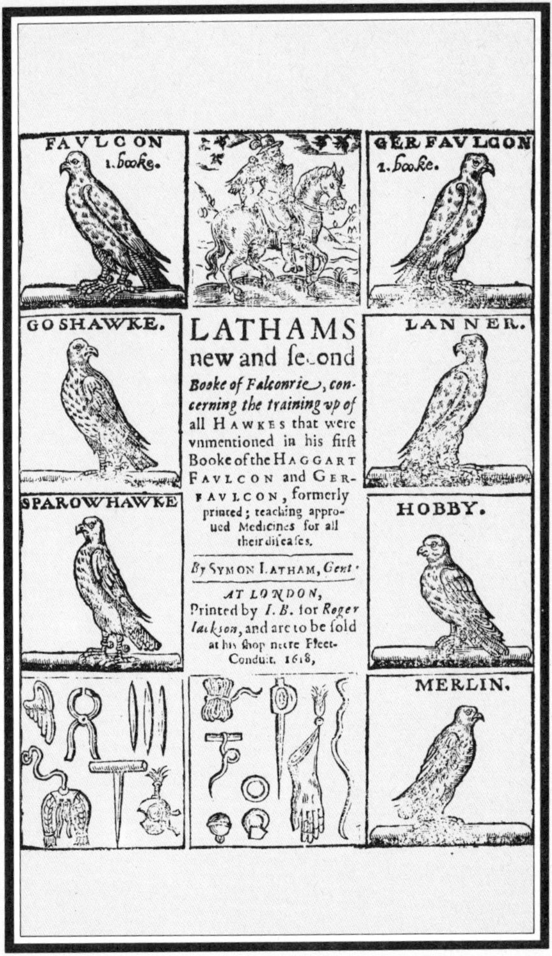
FAVLCON 1. booke.

GER FAVLCON 1. booke.

GOSHAWKE.

LANNER.

SPAROWHAWKE

HOBBY.

MERLIN.

LATHAMS new and second Booke of Falconrie, concerning the training vp of all HAWKES that were vnmentioned in his first Booke of the HAGGART FAVLCON and GERFAVLCON, formerly printed; teaching approued Medicines for all their diseases.

By SYMON LATHAM, Gent.

AT LONDON, Printed by I. B. for Roger Iackson, and are to be sold at his shop neere Fleet-Conduit. 1618,

Lord and master of all the island birds, the magnificent peregrine falcon hunted starling, duck and wading bird, rising high for the deadly power stoop and striking each victim dead in mid-air with one blow of clenched talons. The little merlin came and stayed awhile, to chase the pipits and larks with tenacious twists and turns, until a frantic quarry miscalculated the last aerial trick. Now and then a migrating sparrowhawk flew in; its tactics were to beat swiftly and low over the ground, to flush some small bird, and sweep it up before it could gather its wings properly. The slow-moving kestrel hovered precisely on the sea-wind as if pinned to the sky; I saw it plummet upon mouse, beetle, worm or insect in the heather, then move to a fresh station in mid-air.

Buzzards were my daily companions, like lesser eagles soaring on broad pinions from one outcrop of rock to another. Leisurely in flight, majestic and dignified, they were cunning to seize any prey by surprise - a young crow foolishly absorbed in its daily bath, a frog or a slow-worm incautiously slipping through the grass, even worms in the dew. As vultures clear up carrion, my buzzards dealt with nature's casualities - the migratory bird battered by weather and too tired to move after crossing the sea, the sick rabbit, and the rabbit itself helplessly struggling in a snare.

R. M. LOCKLEY
THE ISLAND

PLATE 4.

PEREGRINE FALCON

'*Queen.* Believe me, lords, for flying at the brook,
I saw not better sport these seven years' day:
Yet, by your leave, the wind was very high;
And, ten to one, old Joan had not gone out.
King. But what a point, my lord, your falcon made,
And what a pitch she flew above the rest! -
To see how God in all his creatures works!
Yea, man and birds are fain of climbing high.
Suff. No marvel, an it like your majesty,
My lord protector's hawks do tower so well;
They know their master loves to be aloft,
And bears his thoughts above his falcon's pitch.
Glo. My lord, 'tis but a base ignoble mind
That mounts no higher than a bird can soar.
Card. I thought as much; he'd be above the clouds.

SHAKESPEARE
HENRY VI, Pt II

I take the sandy path that goes
Across the moors: on this most bitter day
A rosette of fallen feathers shows
That a high hawk went hunting here;
And in this strange and winter landscape,
With dry leaves on huckleberry and bay,
The torn victim that did not escape,
Is brilliant suddenly, a flower's display.
I see the foliage in the wings,
That cup cheek-feathers and soft down,
As blossoms, but a gust flings
My fancy wide: so rudely blown
The feathers are only those of a dead bird,
And overhead the hunting hawk still swings.
Ignoring my fancy, so personal and absurd,
It scans the moors, to see what bareness brings.

RUTHVEN TODD
THE HAWK'S VICTIM

Serenely far there swam in the sunny height
A buzzard and his mate who took their pleasure
Swirling and poising idly in golden light:
On great pied motionless moth-wings borne along,
  So effortless and so strong,
Cutting each other's paths, together they glided,
Then wheeled asunder till they soared divided
Two valleys wideth (as though it were delight
To part like this, being sure they could untie
So swiftly in their empty, free dominion),
Curved headlong downward, towering up the
  sunny steep,
Then with a sudden lift of the one great pinion,
Swung proudly to a curve and from its height
Took half a mile of sunlight in one long sweep.

MARTIN ARMSTRONG
BUZZARDS

Litho. W. Greve, Berlin.

HONEY-BUZZARD.

Pernis apivorus (Linn.)

I am a wind on the sea,
I am a wave of the ocean,
I am the roar of the sea,
I am a powerful ox,
I am a hawk on a cliff.

AMERGIN'S CHANT
BOOK OF INVASIONS

Illustration acknowledgements

5 Imperial Eagle © *India Office Library*

7 Hawk on Glove: Maj. Gen. Hardwicke. 'Drawings of Birds of India' © *Natural History Museum*

9 Raider over London: C. F. Tunnicliffe © *Mrs Dorothy Downes from estate of the late C. F. Tunnicliffe*

11 Kestrel: J. Gould 'Birds of Great Britain' © *Alan Spain*

13 A Boy with a Hawk and Leash: J. Van Noordt. *From the Wallace Collection*

15 Goshawk: Jean Wolf 'Oiseaux de l'Allemagne' © *Natural History Museum*

17 Greenland Falcon: J. Gould 'Birds of Great Britain' © *C. H. Sotheran Ltd*

19 Hawk on Rock in Stream: Finger painting by Kao Ch'i-p'ei, Chinese 18th Century. *Paul G. Moss Collection*

21 The Crested or Coped Black Vulture and Black and White Snake: G. Edwards – *Thomas Pennant's Genera of Birds*

23 Vulture: *French print from original by Paquien 19th Century.* © *Baynton – Williams*

25 Over St Johns Hill: Ceri Richards © *Mrs Rachel Patterson*

The author and publisher gratefully acknowledge the following for permission to use copyright material:

Jonathan Cape Ltd for 'The Goshawk' by T. H. White; William Collins Ltd for 'The Peregrine' by J. A. Baker; J. M. Dent Ltd for 'The Hawk's Victim' by Ruthven Todd; Andre Deutsch Ltd for R. M. Lockley's 'The Island'; Gerald Duckworth for Hilaire Belloc's 'The Vulture'; Faber and Faber Ltd for Herbert Read's 'The Falcon and the Dove' from *Collected Poems* and Ted Hughes's 'Hawk Roosting' from *Lupercal*; David Higham Associates, J. M. Dent Ltd and the trustees for the Dylan Thomas Estate for 'Over Sir John's Hill' from *Collected Poems* and Macmillan and Co. Ltd for 'The Hawk' by W. B. Yeats.

The author also acknowledges the assistance of Dr Ann Ross of Southampton University, the staff at the National Library of Wales, Mrs Phyllis Clifton and Fred Read.